Harriet Tubman

A Buddy Book
by
Randy T. Gosda

ABDO
Publishing Company

VISIT US AT

www.abdopub.com

Published by Buddy Books, an imprint of ABDO Publishing Company, 4940 Viking Drive, Suite 622, Edina, Minnesota 55435. Copyright © 2002 by Abdo Consulting Group, Inc. International copyrights reserved in all countries. No part of this book may be reproduced in any form without written permission from the publisher.

Printed in the United States.

Edited by: Christy DeVillier
Contributing Editors: Matt Ray, Michael P. Goecke
Image Research: Deborah Coldiron, Susan Will
Graphic Design: Jane Halbert
Cover Photograph: North Wind Picture Archives
Interior Photographs/Illustrations: North Wind Picture Archives, Library of Congress, Deborah Coldiron, Corbis

Library of Congress Cataloging-in-Publication Data

Gosda, Randy T., 1959-
    Harriet Tubman / Randy T. Gosda.
        p. cm. — (First biographies. Set II)
    Includes index.
    Summary: Surveys the life of Harriet Tubman, who spent her childhood in slavery and later worked to help other slaves escape north to freedom through the Underground Railroad.
    ISBN 1-57765-736-5
    1. Tubman, Harriet, 1820?-1913—Juvenile literature. 2. Slaves—United States—Biography—Juvenile literature. 3. African American women—Biography—Juvenile literature. 4. African Americans—Biography—Juvenile literature.
    5. Underground railroad—Juvenile literature. [1. Tubman, Harriet, 1820?-1913.
    2. Slaves. 3. African Americans—Biography. 4. Women—Biography. 5. Underground railroad.] I. Title.

E444.T82 G67 2002
973.7'115—dc21
[B]
                                                                    2001034933

Table Of Contents

Who Is Harriet Tubman?

Before 1865, many African Americans lived as slaves in the South. These slaves had no rights and no freedom.

Harriet Tubman believed everyone had the right to be free. She led over 300 slaves to freedom on the Underground Railroad. This brave woman is famous for fighting slavery.

Harriet Tubman

Harriet Tubman's real name was Araminta Ross. But nobody called her that. As a little girl, she was Minty. As a young woman, she was Harriet. Harriet was her mother's name.

Harriet And Her Family

Harriet Tubman was born around 1820 in Maryland. Back then, Maryland was a slave state. Harriet and her family were slaves.

Edward Brodas owned Harriet and her family. They worked on Mr. Brodas's plantation. A plantation is a large farm.

Harriet had 10 brothers and sisters. Harriet's big family lived in a small cabin. This cabin had one room and no windows. Harriet and her family slept on a dirt floor.

Harriet's first home may have looked like this old slave cabin.

Growing Up

One day, Mr. Brodas sent Harriet away. She started working for the Cook family. Young Harriet helped Mrs. Cook make cloth. She helped Mr. Cook trap muskrats. This was hard work for seven-year-old Harriet.

Many slaves like Harriet worked hard picking cotton.

Harriet missed her family. The Cooks did not give her much to eat. Harriet got very sick. So, the Cooks sent her back to Mr. Brodas.

Slave Life

Slave life was very hard. Harriet cleaned houses. She picked cotton. Someone punished Harriet when she made a mistake. Harriet could not go to school. Harriet hated being a slave. But she could not quit working for Mr. Brodas.

One day, Harriet saw a slave run away. The overseer chased the runaway slave. Harriet followed. The overseer threw a heavy weight at the runaway slave. But the weight hit Harriet in the head. This hurt Harriet badly. It left a scar on her head.

It was not easy to run away from slavery.

The runaway slave gave Harriet an idea. Harriet thought about running away from Mr. Brodas's plantation.

Harriet heard people talk about the Underground Railroad. This was not a real railroad with a train. The Underground Railroad was made up of people. These people knew slavery was wrong. The Underground Railroad secretly helped slaves run away to freedom.

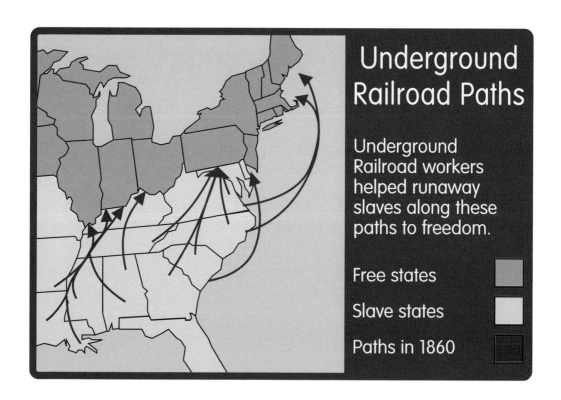

Underground Railroad Paths

Underground Railroad workers helped runaway slaves along these paths to freedom.

Free states

Slave states

Paths in 1860

Harriet married John Tubman in 1844. John Tubman used to be a slave. John's owner set him free. Harriet wanted to be free like John. She talked to John about running away. But John thought running away was a bad idea.

The Way To Freedom

In 1849, Harriet Tubman secretly ran away. She did not tell her family or John Tubman.

Harriet went to a woman of the Underground Railroad. She told Harriet how to find the next station. A station was a safe hiding place for runaway slaves.

Runaway slaves could rest at Underground Railroad stations.

Harriet's trip to the North was not easy. Slave hunters were looking for her. She hid during the day. She walked through woods at night. Freedom was 90 miles away.

Finally, Harriet made it to Pennsylvania. Pennsylvania was a free state in the North. Harriet was free!

Runaway slaves often walked through water.
This made it harder for slave hunters to find them.

Another Escape

Runaway slaves often traveled at night.

Harriet lived in Philadelphia. She enjoyed her freedom. She was free to work for herself. She was free to keep the money she earned. But she missed her family.

In Philadelphia, Harriet met the Vigilance Committee. The Vigilance Committee was made up of abolitionists. Abolitionists believed slavery was wrong. The Vigilance Committee helped Harriet. Together, they made plans to set Harriet's family free. In 1850, Harriet went back to Maryland for her family.

The South was full of danger for Harriet. Harriet would be sent back to Mr. Brodas if someone found her. Mr. Brodas would punish her. But Harriet was smart and careful. She dressed up like an old man. She covered the scar on her head. Harriet safely led her family out of the South.

These people escaped slavery with help from Harriet (far left).

Harriet made 18 more trips on the Underground Railroad. Harriet spent 10 years saving these African Americans from slavery. Every person she brought to the North arrived safely. Nobody ever caught Harriet Tubman.

General Tubman

John Andrew was the governor, or leader, of Massachusetts. John Andrew believed Harriet could help the North. The North was fighting the South in the Civil War. John Andrew asked Harriet for her help. She said yes.

Many brave African Americans fought in the Civil War.

Harriet nursed hurt soldiers. She spied on armies. She scouted land. People called Harriet "General Tubman."

Harriet helped the North win the Civil War. Slavery in the United States ended in 1865. Everyone was free!

Helpful Harriet

After the war, Harriet settled in Auburn, New York. She earned money from helping the North. But the United States was slow to pay her.

Being poor did not stop Harriet from helping people. She opened her house to poor and sick people. Harriet never turned anyone away.

Many African Americans had problems after the Civil War. Many did not know how to read or write. Harriet helped them. She raised money to open special schools.

Harriet helped to open schools for African Americans.

In 1870, women did not have the right to vote. Harriet thought this was unfair to women. So, she joined the suffrage movement. Suffragists fought for women's right to vote. Susan B. Anthony was the leader of the suffrage movement.

Susan B. Anthony

Harriet The Brave

   People around the world learned about Harriet Tubman's bravery. Sarah Bradford wrote two books about Harriet's life. The queen of England gave Harriet a Diamond Jubilee Medal.

   Harriet Tubman lived to be 93 years old. Many people today celebrate Harriet's fight against slavery.

Harriet Tubman

Important Dates

1820-21 Harriet Tubman is born around this time.

1844 Harriet marries John Tubman.

1849 Harriet runs away from slavery.

1850 Harriet helps her family escape the South. She works on the Underground Railroad for about 10 years.

1865 "General Tubman" helps the North win the Civil War. The U.S. ends slavery.

1869 Sarah Hopkins Bradford writes *Scenes from the Life of Harriet Tubman*.

1913 Harriet Tubman dies at the age of 93.

March 10, 1990 People celebrate the first Harriet Tubman Day.

Important Words

abolitionist a person who thinks slavery is wrong.

African American an American whose early family members came from Africa.

Civil War the United States war between the Southern states and the Northern states. The North fought the South to end slavery.

overseer a person in charge of others.

scar a mark that stays after healing.

slave a person that can be bought and sold. Many slaves in the United States were African American.

suffrage the right to vote.

Underground Railroad a group of people who helped slaves reach freedom.

Web Sites

Harriet Tubman and the Underground Railroad
www.lhric.org/pocantico/tubman/tubman.html
Compiled by second-graders, this site includes a timeline, puzzles, and photos of Harriet Tubman.

Harriet Tubman
www.pbs.org/wgbh/aia/part4/4p1535.html
This PBS web site offers a detailed biography of Harriet Tubman.

Index